FAMILY

photographs by

LAUREN DUKOFF

foreword by devendra banhart

FaMILY

CHRONICLE BOOKS
San Francisco

for Obi

Library of Congress Cataloging-in-Publication Data:

Dukoff, Lauren.
Family / photographs by Lauren Dukoff ; foreword by Devendra Banhart.
p. cm.
ISBN 978-0-8118-6662-0
1. Musicians-Portraits. 2. Portrait photography. 3. Dukoff, Lauren-Friends and associates. 4. Banhart, Devendra-Friends and associates.
I. Banhart, Devendra. II. Title.

TR681.M86D85 2009
779'.978-dc22

2008046847

Manufactured in China

10 9 8 7 6 5 4 3 2 1

Chronicle Books LLC, 680 Second Street, San Francisco, CA 94107
www.chroniclebooks.com

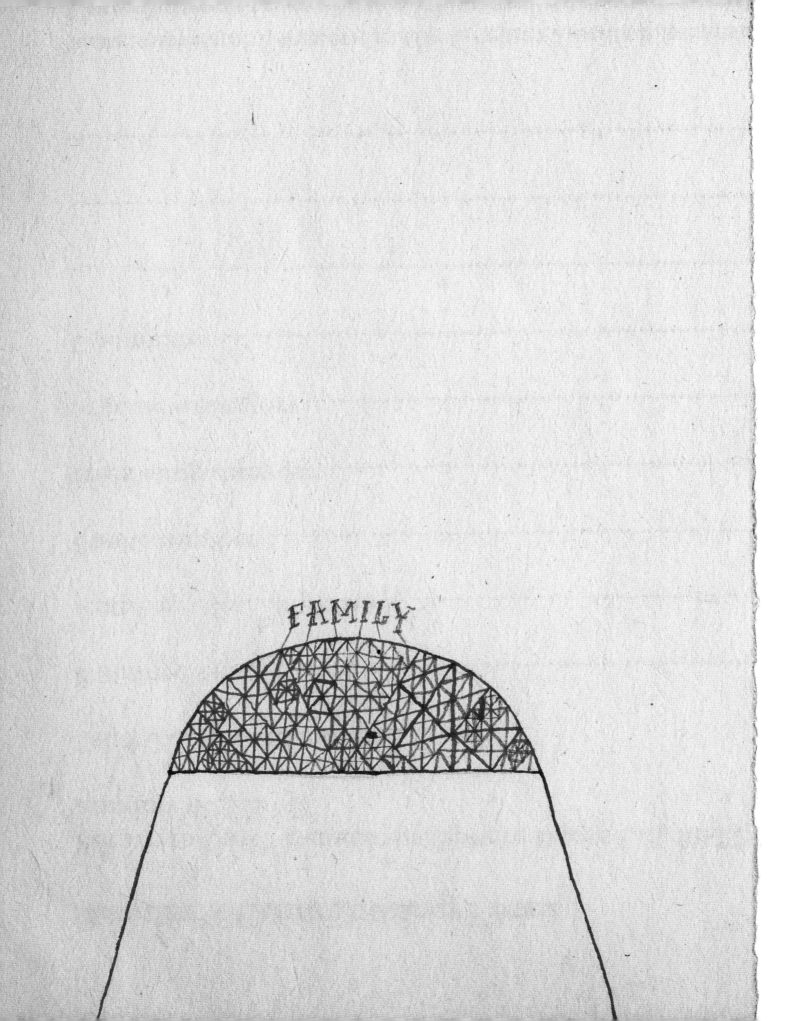

FOREWORD

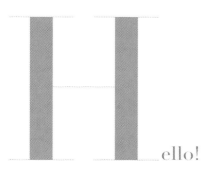ello!

This book is the story of a group of friends, who amongst other things, make music.

Lo is my little sister, not by blood, but by love, and this is her book.

She, amongst other things, is a photographer.

When I moved to America, Lo was one of my first and only friends. I remember driving around L.A. with her, getting lost and listening to music. She was always very clear about what she wanted to do. There was always a camera in her bag.

The lens draws in the light; the eye draws the light in.

All the people in this book knew each other a long, long time ago, from the beginning or somewhere closer to it than today.

I'm in awe of everyone in this book.

I love everyone in this book.

I owe everything to the people in this book.

I tried to write a little paragraph about everyone in this book, but it just didn't feel right. I'm not ready yet. But I am ready to say thank you forever.

I am ready to say that everyone in this book is my family, and my source of inspiration and consolation. My home. One I am taken to every time I listen to one of their plumed tunes.

When I've most needed to hear it (which is all the time) I've heard, "stay open, stay vulnerable, stay strong" from everyone in this book.

But most of all, from Lo.

The heart draws in love. Love draws the heart in.

Thank you forever.

Love above all.

Onward,

—Devendra Banhart
Tuesday afternoon, Bolinas

INTRODUCTION

When I was fourteen years old my father gave me my first camera, a Canon 35mm. I carried it around everywhere I went, and I took pictures incessantly. As soon as I had the camera, I wanted to take pictures of people. I wasn't interested in taking the sorts of pictures that my father, a photographer, was pursuing (abstractions, still lifes, quietly serious images of trees or mountains), and maybe this was in part simply an adolescent urge to go in an opposite direction, but for me when I pointed my lens at a beautiful landscape I felt no sense of excitement or urge to snap away. On the other hand, when I aimed it at a person, I felt as if there was a whole story happening within my frame. A life story—real or imagined—being told with every nuance of expression and every line on a person's face. That's where my passion for taking pictures started to grow from.

Later that year, I wrote an essay on J. D. Salinger's *Nine Stories* for my high school freshman English class. My teacher, Mrs. Gonzalez, said that my writing reminded her of another student of hers, a senior named Devendra. I started spending my lunch hours in Mrs. Gonzalez's classroom, and I guess it was no coincidence that Devendra and his friend Isabelle Albuquerque also spent their lunch hours there. I would read and draw in a sketchbook, and one day Devendra walked over from the other side of the room and said he'd like to see what I was working on.

He was extremely magnetic and charming, and I felt like he and Isabelle were the most beautiful people I'd ever met. At first I wasn't sure what I could possibly contribute. Why were they interested in me? They were four years older, and I felt out of my league, even though at school they were actually on the furthest outer rim of the usual social structure.

Soon, Devendra, Isabelle, and I started to spend many afternoons together riding into the city and wandering the streets. It was then that I began to photograph Devendra and all his friends. The photos were never posed; instead they were simple documentations of our adolescent adventures: shots of trips to the Getty Museum, photographs of Devendra and Isabelle in their backyards, a shot of Devendra through the rearview mirror taken from the backseat, images taken on city buses. These were my first photos.

Just taking pictures of them doing the simplest, everyday things was fascinating for me. It's as if I was studying these older kids—observing and documenting the details.

Ninth graders were not allowed in our high school's darkroom, but one afternoon Devendra and I snuck in and spent a hurried forty-five minutes developing a few prints. The prints were chaos, but there was something there—an excitement in creation and a sure pride in what I'd done, even though many of the photos were blurry and out of focus.

Devendra quickly became like an older brother to me. He started making mix tapes for me even before we'd gotten to know each other very well; tapes full of music I'd never heard before like Donovan, Nick Drake, and Elliott Smith, and readings by Jack Kerouac. He helped open a whole new world of music and creativity for me that helped shape my musical and artistic tastes. Everyone, if they're lucky, has the opportunity to learn from someone just a little older than them. You're not born with slick shoes; someone has to help you pick them out and show you how to tie the laces.

Devendra left for art school in San Francisco after he and Isabelle graduated; I was back for tenth grade, but my friends were gone. I would make the trip up north to visit him whenever I could and was introduced to Noah Georgeson, Joanna Newsom, and Andy Cabic, who to me were just Devendra's friends who happened to make music and art. I had my camera with me at all times, but rarely took any pictures of these new people. I felt like an interloper. I was fifteen years old, lucky just to be hanging out with this group of older artists. The last thing I wanted to do was call attention to myself by bringing my camera out, even as kind and warm as they were to me. But in the safe confines of Devendra's little studio apartment on Columbus St., I was free to snap pictures of him quietly sitting on his bed, strumming his guitar.

Back at home, I would still receive mix tapes from Devendra in the mail. Gradually, the tapes started to include his own songs. He'd always played music—but this was the first time I'd heard actual fully formed songs. Eventually he sent me a tape titled *Oh Me Oh My*—which would later be discovered by Michael Gira and released as Devendra's first album on Young God Records.

Meanwhile, I was feeling more and more out of place at school. After some extensive research and even more extensive pleading with my parents, I took the California High School Proficiency exam and was able to graduate as a junior.

After that I spent a year at Brooks Institute of Photography in Santa Barbara. I spent most of my time in the darkroom but didn't find much pleasure in the college experience. Devendra spent time traveling to Europe and eventually landed in New York. We kept our friendship alive with letters and care packages. The mix tapes did not stop coming; and soon the early songs by his friends like Vetiver, Joanna Newsom, and Bat For Lashes began to appear on these tapes.

In 2006 I was working as studio manager and producer for photographer

Autumn de Wilde. I had admired her work for some time and was really feeling privileged to be able to observe her up close as she shot. I especially loved her documentary-style photos and how she was able to capture musicians in their element, doing what they do. When I mentioned one day that Devendra had been invited to curate and play at one of the three days of music at the All Tomorrow's Parties festival in England, Autumn asked, "Why aren't you going?" I didn't have a good answer.

It was like an epiphany of sorts. I had been shooting Devendra and band-mates for some time—but only as friends. This was the first moment that I realized that I might be able to actually shoot them professionally. After spending so much time watching Autumn document musicians, it had dawned on me that I could photograph Devendra in a similar fashion. I could shoot Devendra and his friends the same way I had in high school; the landscape may have changed—from city buses to tour buses and from backyard to backstage—but the same level of intimacy could remain. It was a turning point in how I saw myself as a photographer because I suddenly realized that people other than myself might be interested in seeing these photos of my friends.

Devendra and I flew into London together and took an incredibly long van ride from the airport to Camber Sands, the seaside resort that had been overtaken by the festival for the weekend. The first day was actually a day off, so I decided to take a bus in to the nearby town of Rye, with Luckey Remington, the bass player in Devendra's band. We wandered through the cobblestone streets and I took pictures. We stood at the top of a hill and watched men bowling on a manicured lawn below us. Sand blew through the streets, creeping up from the beach, and we stood in front of a shop looking at teapots and tin breadboxes behind a window with hand lettering that read "Ironmongers Extraordinary."

While we were waiting outside the train station for a return bus, Ramblin' Jack Elliott appeared on the sidewalk, ten-gallon hat on his head and cravat tied around his neck, his daughter Aiyana standing next to him. We shared a ride back to Camber Sands, and Jack played for a small group of people in our hotel room. He played twelve songs, sitting in a chair in front of a sliding glass door; behind him, through the glass, was the late afternoon and the small courtyard with its low wall. At first I was nervous taking photographs—of Jack, of Devendra with his eyes closed listening to the music—but I knew I would never forgive myself if I didn't capture this moment. I found a new sense of comfort taking pictures that evening. I could hide behind my camera and put all my attention into the picture-taking process.

Devendra moved back to Los Angeles in 2006 and shared a little house in Venice with Noah Georgeson and Matteah Baim. With Devendra back in town, we could see more of each other, but in meeting Matteah I also found a great photographic muse. We went together to the Getty Center to see Vashti Bunyan play while I took quick pictures—photos were not allowed—and the audience clapped over the sounds of my shutter. Matteah was writing and recording her album *Death of the Sun* at the time and asked me to play flute on one of her songs and take some photos. On New Year's Day we went to Malibu, and I photographed her throwing her guitar over the cliff, a picture she later chose for the cover of her album. During that same period, I shot Noah as he was finishing up his album *Find Shelter*, and I also was invited to come and shoot pictures of Isabelle and Jon Beasley, who had just formed the band Hecuba. Isabelle and Jon wanted formal-style portraits taken, so I brought my 4 × 5 camera, which I had learned how to use while at Brooks. It felt as if everything was coming together. There was so much creativity coming out of this circle of people, and I was feeling fortunate to be there in the middle of it all to take pictures.

I began to travel more to take pictures, realizing, obviously, that if I was going to try to capture these artists in the moment, I would have to try to be there when those moments occurred. So I went to Chicago in 2006 for the Pitchfork Festival, where Devendra and Priestbird were playing. Andy Cabic and the rest of the guys from Vetiver made a detour from their tour to come hang out, and Andy joined Devendra on stage. It was an especially hot July and the record-breaking heat and humidity kept fogging my lens and made it nearly impossible to take any good pictures outside. In the interest of being anywhere with air-conditioning, Devendra and I took a cab to a western boot store that Matteah had told me about. Their claim to fame was that they had made custom boots for Andre the Giant, which were there on display, enormous and amazing. We wandered through the aisles, and I took pictures of Devendra—surrounded by what seemed like an inordinate number of boots.

Somewhere around this time, I had begun to find myself doing more and more professional photography. I was starting to shoot other artists, actors, and models, and my work was starting to appear in more press and on album packaging and the like, but I still felt most connected to my extended group of friends.

In October of 2006, I went to San Francisco to photograph Devendra, who was performing at Neil Young's Bridge School Benefit. With my Mamiya 645, I took my place in the designated photographer's pit, an area that I was becoming familiar with. I was shooting film, like I always had (and still do), and I remember how the other photographers in the photo pit, with their enormous digital cameras, made a point of mocking me as I kept changing rolls. But it didn't matter. There were Neil Young and my friends on stage together! Matteah, Eliza Douglas, Andy

Cabic, Pete Newsom, Otto Hauser, Luckey, Benjamin Oak Goodman, Devendra, and Bert Jansch had all joined Neil and were up there singing "Rockin' in the Free World." After the show, Matteah described the experience of looking down from the stage: "There's twenty thousand people, and there's Lo."

In 2007 Devendra rented a house at the top of a hill in Topanga while he was recording *Smokey Rolls Down Thunder Canyon*, and I would drive up there as often as I could to see what they were up to. There was a steep driveway and a porch and two stovepipe chimneys that poked out from the roof. The walls were wood paneled and the second floor walls were mostly windows that looked out onto an endless spray of trees.

The house was littered with the usual band member paraphernalia—empty liquor bottles, instrument cables, candles, ashtrays—but mixed in was a collection of mysteriously valuable rock 'n' roll totems: a burgundy velvet couch that had once belonged to Jim Morrison, Mick Jagger's suit, Bob Dylan's hat.

They all lived and slept in the house for months, inviting friends up to come and play. Rodrigo Amarante, Vashti Bunyan, Matteah Baim, Linda Perhacs, Chris Robinson, Otto Hauser, Gael Garcia Bernal, and Benjamin Oak Goodman all stopped by to contribute to the recordings. The usual suspects—Luckey Remington, Greg Rogove, Noah Georgeson, Andy Cabic, and Pete Newsom—were always there as well. There were boys coming out of every crevice of that house. A tent out on the front deck held the spillover when there was no more room to sleep on the floor inside. No one ever seemed to have shoes on. I would come up to the house, expecting to stay for two hours, and end up spending the entire day, filling my bags with rolls and rolls of shot film. There was always something going on, and once I was there I was afraid that if I left, I might miss something.

It was around this time that I began to get the feeling that the photos I had been taking were beginning to tell a larger story. I'd started off photographing Devendra, which led to photographing his friends and the people he was making music with, and those people led me to more people and the music they were making. As if this community of artists was forming a sort of family tree of like-minded individuals. A sort of extended family, tied together, not necessarily by their musical sounds, but by shared ideas and influences and a mutual admiration for each other. Although Devendra's music was different from Matteah's, and Matteah's was different from Bat For Lashes, or Espers, or Vetiver, there was clearly a commonality that tied them together. I decided that I needed to go further to document this group of musicians, to follow each branch of this makeshift family tree as far as it would take me.

So, with a little help from Devendra, I mapped out a plan to visit and photograph the musicians that I didn't know quite as well, but who seemed to be crucial members of this group, in one way or another. I imagined that these photo sessions would probably end up being brief and to the point, more "professional"—seeing as these were not people who were already friends of mine. Instead they ended up being long afternoons of hanging out, talking, laughing, and eating. I was welcomed into people's homes and into their most intimate spaces as if I were a relative. The amount of warmth and trust I was given was truly touching and truly served to solidify the feeling that was, without a doubt, a sort of family.

In New York I photographed Natasha Kahn (of Bat For Lashes) in the Brooklyn apartment she'd recently moved into, which had belonged to a woman who'd passed away, unpacked boxes lining the walls and old fabric curtains in her window fluttering in the breeze.

I took the bus upstate to visit Priestbird at the small house near Woodstock where they were recording rough takes for their next album. Greg met me at the bus stop and we took photos by a small barn behind the house, surrounded by half a dozen goats and kids and one bucking male goat who was itching for a challenge.

In Philadelphia I rushed to shoot as many pictures of the members of Espers as I could in the fading afternoon light in Helena Espvall's lovely tiled courtyard. Once all the natural light was gone, we moved inside and I photographed the band gathered together in her warm, cozy kitchen. Afterward I shared sushi with Helena and Brooke Sietinsons at a nearby Japanese restaurant.

In Baltimore I met up with Jana Hunter and had afternoon drinks before we went back to the Hopkins Inn where I was staying. The turn-of-the-century building was eerily quiet, and as I shot her climbing the main stairwell, the noise from my camera's shutter echoed loudly off the walls.

I met Cibelle in her flat in East London, which felt like it was overflowing with artwork and trinkets and an unending supply of items you wanted to stop and look more closely at. We shared a cup of tea in her kitchen, where she told me how she and Devendra had bonded over their love for Caetano Veloso when they first met in Paris. Then I took pictures of her as we walked through Dalston Market, where she and Devendra had filmed the video for her song "London, London."

The walls of Vashti Bunyan's Edinburgh home were covered with photographs—pictures of her children and of Vashti as a child. There were piles of quilts and linens, freshly washed and stacked in a laundry basket. She showed me posters and memorabilia she had collected and letters from Devendra. Vashti romanticized America and the energy of New York, while I was rapt and romanticizing Edinburgh and Vashti's warm, quiet existence.

At home in Los Angeles, I visited Guy Blakeslee in Laurel Canyon. His backyard spilled out into a canyon, and we walked out and up a dangerous hillside to a little bench among the trees. We talked about Guy's first tour with Devendra, and he showed me his copy of the *Psychedelic Encyclopedia*. A few days later, I was on the other side of the hills, riding through Topanga Canyon with Linda Perhacs, the Godmother of psychedelia. She wanted to re-create the cover of her album *Parallelograms*, and I took pictures of her walking through tall grass. She told me that she could see music visually. That she'd been driving down this very road when visions of shapes and colors came to her. Pulling over to the side of the road, she began to sketch what she saw, drawing out the sounds of that album. "Ever since I was a little girl," she said, "I could see music in a three-dimensional form." I told her that I was working on a book that would document the experiences I'd had among a group of friends and like-minded musicians. She said, "The connections in your book follow something that's beyond the pedestrian plain."

For a long time, I thought that one's job as a photographer was to stay the hell out of the way. To retreat to a safe distance and act as a voyeur, always being careful to never let yourself get caught up in the moment that you're capturing, thereby altering it. I was wrong. Now I don't think that you can ever fully disengage from your subject, and I'm not sure that much good would arise from doing so. Looking back on how I started taking pictures of my friends, I realize that, in truth, I always was a part of those moments. I have always been a part of this circle of friends, not just an outsider documenting them.

Over the course of putting this book together, as the circle of people I was photographing expanded concentrically, I feel that I have been incredibly fortunate to have been allowed to participate in so many important moments in people's lives—in their recording sessions, on stage, in their kitchens, and in their bedrooms. They welcomed me into their most intimate spaces. I consider them my friends, even my extended family. It is the stories we've shared and the conversations we've had that produced these images. Thank you.

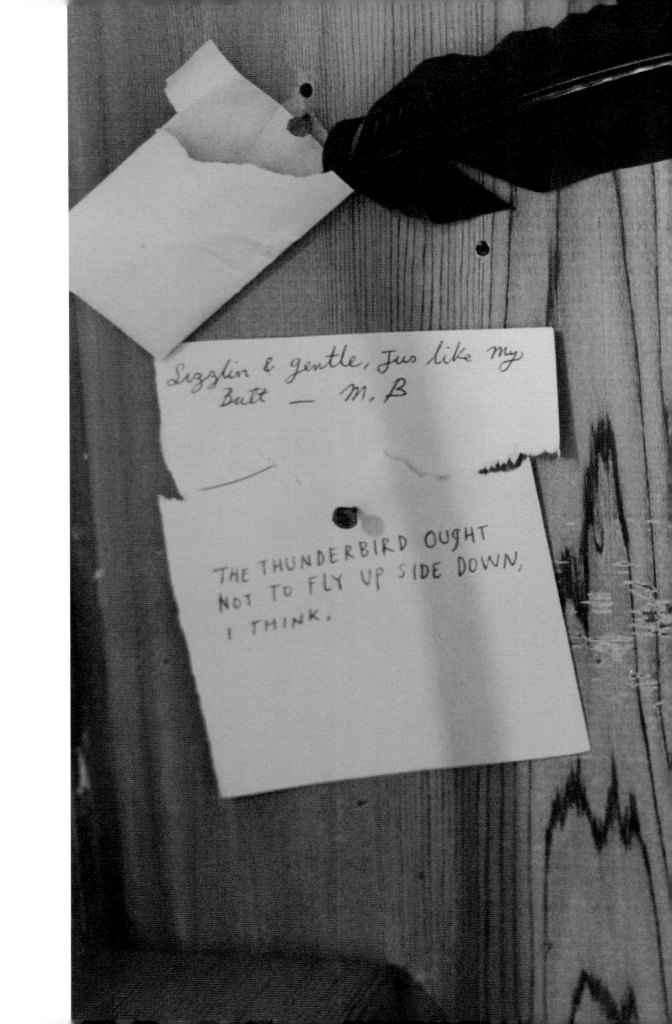

I
EVEN I
MUST DIE SOMETIME
SO OF WHAT VALUE
IS ANYTHING
I THINK

— WINNEBAGO
SONG

ALL TOMORROWS PARTIES
SUNDAY 14TH MAY 2006

Stage One

Doors › 3.30pm
TARANTULA A.D › 4.00pm – 4.45pm
METALLIC FALCONS › 5.15pm – 6.00pm
ESPERS › 6.30pm – 7.15pm
VETIVER › 7.45pm – 8.30pm
BERT JANSCH › 9.00pm – 9.45pm
VASHTI BUNYAN › 10.15pm – 11.00pm
DEVENDRA BANHART › 11.30pm – 1.00am

Stage Two

Doors › 2.30pm
DANIELLE STECH HOMSY › 3.15pm – 4.00pm
BAT FOR LASHES › 4.30pm – 5.15pm
JANA HUNTER › 5.45pm – 6.30pm
SPLEEN › 7.00pm – 7.45pm
JANDEK › 8.30pm – 9.45pm
RAMBLIN JACK ELLIOTT › 10.15pm – 11.15pm

DJ ZACH COWIE (DRAG CITY)
+ GUESTS 1.00am – 5.00am

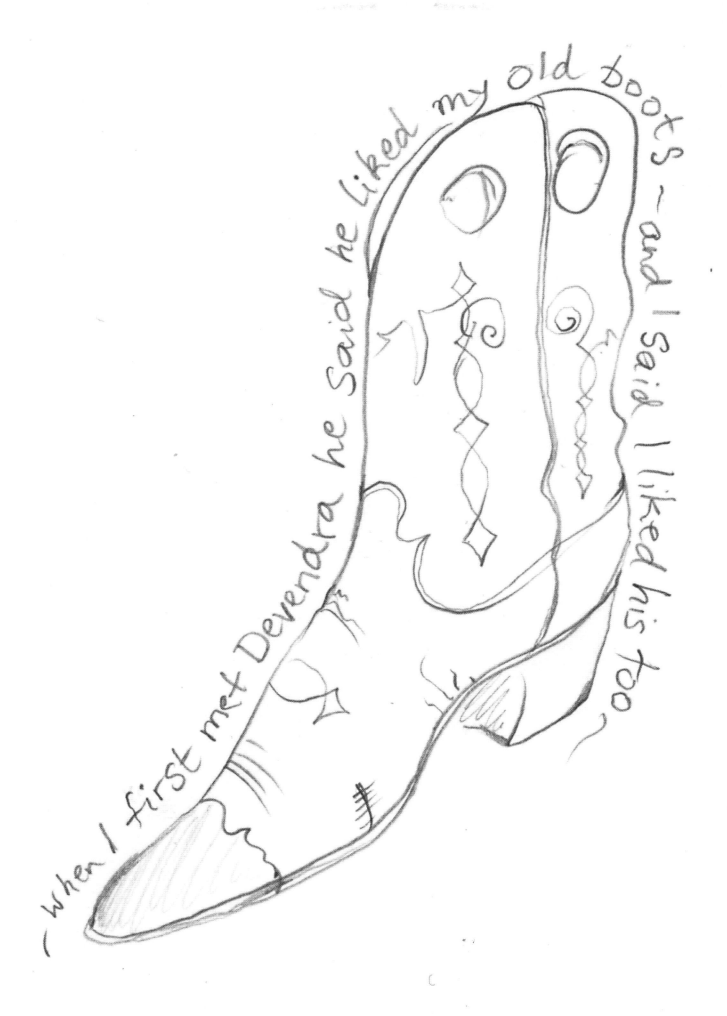

When I first met Devendra he said he liked my old boots ~ and I said I liked his too

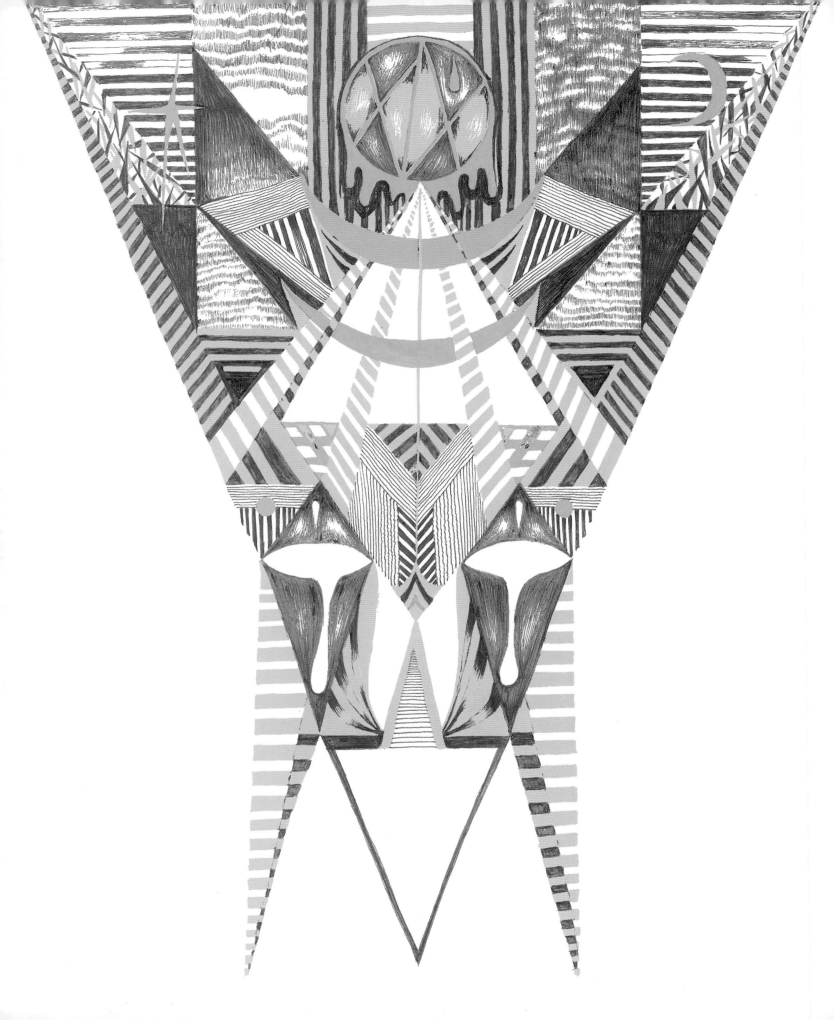

UNTITLED
Isabelle Albuquerque

I was with my sister and we were climbing over a fence.
It was pitch black, on a road with no street lamps.
And then appeared the headlights of a car.
Inside were two beautiful Venezuelan women and a boy.
He was going by the name "The Christmas Spirit" then.
We took him with us down another dark road with no street
lamps
to the lake.
We had to walk for about a mile from the road to get to the
water.
There were pockets of warm air in an otherwise cold
California desert night.
We walked in and out of the warm spaces,
like swimming in the ocean through places where people
may have peed.
He had white specks stuck in his fingernails
from white paint
from white out
wipe out
white markings that covered hundreds of paintings and
manila envelopes that were lying in stacks back at his home
on the unlit road.
He was the Christmas Spirit. And he was also Obi.
He talked for hours about a book he was reading where all
the animals could speak.
Maybe it was an animal play.
We said goodbye and went to bed.
Soon after I would walk down this road
and it would be day then and the black asphalt too hot to
walk barefoot on
and I discovered that the fence to his house had a button
hidden behind a post that would open it up
and often even before I pushed the button I could hear
singing, echoing throughout the canyon.
Sometimes beautiful, sometimes the way that the coyotes
yell when they have caught a rabbit.
Or maybe it is the rabbit yelling then.
We watched movies and made graffiti in a strip mall where
nobody noticed.
We met Lo.
We met Ajit.

We met Anti.
We drove to San Francisco falling in love with the all the
women who worked at the drive-throughs for McDonald's
that lay up and down the one freeway to the 110 to the 5.
He started to sing in other places besides through the
mountain:
On the answering machine, four track, the smell.
One night a man yelled "you suck" over and over as he
played.
Anti had paid the man to do that.
The music was something very special to see. To hear.
It kind of stopped you dead.

We were 18 or maybe 17.
I moved to New York and Obi moved to San Francisco.
I didn't know a single soul in the city.
On my birthday he sent a huge package:
Japanese candies, drawings, and most special, a tape with
new songs and some things spoken.
I went to San Francisco.
I met Noah.
I met Sarah.
I met Andy.
Obi came to New York.
I stayed with him for one week in an old abandoned build-
ing that he was squatting in at the end of a small street in
Brooklyn.
He had filled the crumbling room with photographs and
drawings.
I had no place to stay and he invited me into the place
where he had no place to stay.
I remember feeling so grateful for his hospitality.
He worked as a bus boy at a fancy vegetarian restaurant in
the city
and would bring home food in paper cartons to share.
The Christmas Spirit.
The police came to the abandoned building and he talked
them away.
He was Devendra then.
There was a performance there, with Devendra and my
good friend at the time who was going by a name that I

don't remember. Something to do with the sunset.
She sang all her songs a capella and I remember standing with her outside while she warmed up her voice before the show.

There were more shows. In one at a beautiful place that is no longer there called Tonic, Devendra played one of the most moving sets I had ever seen. And then he went down to basement and shaved off his beard and put on a dress and walked right back on stage to do another show as the lead diva in the terrific band Abra.
Other people were craning their necks to see and hear now.
It was the kind of night that made you cry.
I met Antony.
His art, too, cut through everything else.
I was with Jon then. It was during the time that was our beginning.

Matteah was also there.
One day we laid with our backs against the wooden floor in her apartment in Greenpoint and listened to Led Zeppelin records for hours.
It was like heaven.

Jon and I went back to California.
The West.
We began to make our own music.
Lo had been living in the hills in Echo Park.
We picked up where we had left off.
She started to change the way that I saw photography and she took pictures for our new music.
It felt right.
Devendra came, too.
The West.
He curated a show called Hypnorituals and Mesmemusical Miracles Hanging in the Sky at a club on Sunset Blvd.
called El Cid.
We played the only four songs that we knew.
I met Erica.
I met Adam.
I met Ariana.
Devendra introduced so many friends.

He was traveling all over the world then
and I couldn't see him as much
but often how he was doing
what he was up to, could be found in the new songs.
In October he asked Jon and me to open for Hairy Fairy in Phoenix
Tuscon
California.
He traveled with a pack of brothers
Andy
Noah
Luckey
Greg
Pete.
They are all incredible men and musicians.
We ended in Los Angeles at the Orpheum Theatre.
Judy Garland had sang there.
Another gift.
At one point during the Hairy Fairy show,
Lo and I stepped outside for a smoke.
For a few minutes it was quiet.
Then from the alleyway we heard shouts and felt trembling.
Lo grabbed her camera and was ushered inside.
I followed and could see that the huge ancient stage was shaking.
Hundreds and hundreds of kids had rushed it.
The fire marshal had been called
and the club owners were threatening to shut down the place down before it fell down.
It was the end of a long tour for the band of brothers.
The first tour for us.
The kids were yelling and stomping and laughing.
Lo was taking pictures
and Devendra was shouting
"It's not illegal to dance.
It's not illegal to dance."

IN TWO TOWARDS
Kevin Barker

to travel towards the setting sun prolongs the dusk
to pick apart a beating heart dispels the lust
embark upon the ark
noah, lonely man
travel in two towards
a warmer, drier land

(for chuck)

WE CAME HOME
Ariana Delawari

Up through the war
through darker days a movement born
we came home

home to our souls
a force of love so bright and bold
we came home

we were runnin free
catchin the waves of the unknown
we came home

a nation born
of immigration must let go
of the throne

we were runnin free
catchin the waves of the unknown
we came home

out in that storm
our songs made rainbows so they'd know
the way home

like our heroes
who sang in rain and moved our souls
so we'd know
the way home
we came home
we came home.

(May 2008)

SIGMUND AND
THE FATHER OF LIES

Ruthann Friedman

a satchel of demons,
red-eyed fork tongued,
gather from musty corners,
lie in wait
burn midnight oil,
tie shoelaces together
light matches between
sock and sole.

baton wielding denizens,
legacy twirling menaces,
they witness
this bent back submission,
this forehead creasing homage to
the family tar baby.

fist follows fist
sinking deeper into
the sludge index
finger, wrist, forearm, elbow, armpit,
the greater the struggle
the stucker you get.

I have been stripped
naked analyzed,
shouted at in morning's first light
and whimpered into moonless skies.

still
while I slouch here
on this upholstered plastic chair-in-a-row.
while I await boarding instructions
for flight #801 to Pittsburg,
I hear terrible trophies poking around
sticking stiletto pinky claws
into worn valise latches.

FROM THE BRIDGE SCHOOL
Matteah Baim

BEING A BROKEN ARROW makes you happy.
The happy I imagine you feel coming upon an oasis in the
desert. It's the house that music built. When you walk inside,
you can feel the blood in your veins begin to hum a tune.
Outside, there's a tree, a fire, Neil Young, Peggy Young, their
daughter laughing. It was too much for a guy like me. I cried
on the pathway.

IN THE UPSTAIRS BATHROOM of the ranch, there are
the most amazing pictures of the most amazing folks.
Among the greats, one stood out to my eye. It glowed with
a gentle light of its own. There was Brian Jones standing
alone . . . looking through the camera at me.

ONE MORNING BRIAN WILSON was sitting in the lobby
of our hotel. A Beach Boys song happened to come on the
radio. Nothing happened. A guy came up to him and told
him he liked his shirt. It was just a regular sort of shirt.

A MEMORABLE SOUND CHECK is a rare and fine thing.
The sounds move around like ghosts beautifully haunting
an abandoned town. On the first morning of Bridge School.
I was trying out my mic. Bert Jansch started playing along
with me. For a moment, we serenaded the amphitheater
1,000s of times empty and full of music.

ROCKIN' IN THE FREE WORLD ended the show each
night. Everyone who had performed was supposed to be on
stage. I had planned on being far, far, far in the back, but
Elliot pushed me right out front. I found myself face-to-face
with a crowd on its feet, arms up for Neil Young. Some how
I spotted Lauren down below taking pictures. I remember
thinking to myself, "There's 20,000 people and Lo."

E-MAIL
Devendra Banhart and Vashti Bunyan

friday july 6th 2001

oh my god, what a day i just cant believe it.

hello, my name is devendra banhart, im a little tick from san francisco, here in paris to play music, on a pirate boat! i first heard about your album a few years ago, i dont know why and damn it its no joke, it just stayed with me, something said, you have to find this you have to find this, finally i did, in paris! thank you so much, its in my little room with John Hurt, Leadbelly, Willie Johnson, Fred McDowell, Memphis Minnie, Mr Drake, Os Mutantes, etc., the special room, the healing; the comfort room, thank you room, and the strength room.

everyday I want to give up playing shows and everyday I know I cant, its contradictory and absurd but maybe you know what im saying? Miss Bunyan, I cant believe you wrote back, I thank you for that, I want to make this short, a short email because electronic communication is strange and its even stranger to be communicating with someone whose music has been so precious to me and all the people I have shared it with, I would like to send you a recording of my music and a small book of poetry, I completely understand if you are unwilling to disclose any address where you might receive something from a stranger, in any case, god damn I thank you with my heart, Devendra Obi Banhart.

sunday july 8th 2001

Hello Devendra

DON'T call yourself a little tick—I'm sure you're not—anyone who can perform and make music is NOT a little tick believe me.

I am about to embark upon performing for the first time in 30 years and I am so scared I can't tell you, so I admire any-one who can get up in front of a whole load of people and perform.

I'll ask my label Spinney if I can give their address to you.

I'm grateful that you like the music I made all those years ago and that it speaks to you now.

Always amazing to me.

Best wishes to you

Vashti

(a package arrived at Spinney Records, where it stayed on a desk a few months)

monday 26th november 2001

Hello there Devendra

Thank you for the package. Paul Lambden was intrigued by the envelope.

I ABSOLUTELY LOVE YOUR WORK, YOUR STYLE AND YOUR INVENTION.

Please go on as you are, I think you will find much success and happiness in what you do.

I hope you have found a place to live by now.

I was in LA visiting my son Leif twice this year. He is trying to be an actor having gone there 11 years ago to be that—and going all kinds of other paths before coming back full circle to what he really wants to do.

Meantime he had some adventures—a lot of which he won't tell me about but only his sister—who tells me.

I will play your music to my daughter who is still quite near to me. She will like it as I do I think. She is a painter.

I know she will like the poems book too but I will always keep it.

Thank you for entrusting me with them.

I am very happy

Love Vashti xxxxxxxxx

BIOGRAPHIES

Matteah Baim

Matteah Baim was born and raised in Milwaukee, Wisconsin. When she was thirteen, she purchased her first guitar and first record, the Doors bootleg *Whiskey, Mystics and Men*, from a basement pawn shop. In 1996 at the age of seventeen, Baim moved to California to study painting and drawing at the San Francisco Art Institute. After graduating, she moved to New York City, where she met Sierra Casady. In 2005 the duo began to write music together and formed the self-described "soft-metal band" Metallic Falcons. Their 2006 debut, *Desert Doughnuts*, was recorded in Brooklyn, Chicago, and New Mexico and featured appearances by Antony Hegarty, Devendra Banhart, Jana Hunter, and Greg Rogove. After only a few live performances, Metallic Falcons disbanded. Shortly thereafter, Baim moved to Los Angeles, where she began writing and recording material for her first solo record, *Death of the Sun*, released on Dicristina Stairbuilders in 2007. Baim continued to tour and also wrote and recorded material for her second solo record, *Laughing Boy*, which was released in January 2009. The album features performances by Butchy Fuego, Robert A. A. Lowe, Leyna Papach, Rob Doran, Emmett Kelly, Hisham Bharoocha, Birdie Lawson, and Rose Lazar. Baim lives and works in New York.

Devendra Banhart

Born in Houston, Texas, in 1981, Devendra Banhart moved with his mother to Caracas, Venezuela, when he was two years old. Eleven years later, his mother remarried, and the family moved to Encinal Canyon in California, where Banhart learned English and began to play music. After attending the San Francisco Art Institute for a year, he dropped out to begin a nomadic period, moving from Los Angeles to Paris to San Francisco to New York and then back to Los Angeles, all the while writing and playing music. At the age of twenty-one, then homeless, Devendra was discovered by Michael Gira, former frontman of the legendary New York group Swans and owner of Young God Records. Gira had received a tape of Banhart's crudely recorded songs, which he decided to release as is. This became the critically acclaimed 2002 album *Oh Me Oh My*. In 2003, Banhart toured North America with Entrance and Gira's band Angels of Light, and in 2004 released the albums *Rejoicing in the Hands* and *Niño Rojo*. A vocal champion of the underexposed musicians who preceded him, Banhart cites artists such as Karen Dalton, Linda Perhacs, and Vashti Bunyan as inspirations. He has generously supported his contemporaries as well, releasing with *Arthur Magazine* the 2004 compilation *Golden Apples of the Sun*, which included the musicians Vetiver, Joanna Newsom, Espers, Jana Hunter, Kevin Barker, and Entrance. In 2005 Banhart released the album *Cripple Crow*, followed by *Smokey Rolls Down Thunder Canyon* in 2008, the latter album crafted with musical collaborators Noah Georgeson, Luckey Remington, Greg Rogove, Andy Cabic, Rodrigo Amarante, and Pete Newsom. Banhart played at the 2006 music festivals Coachella and Bonnaroo, and curated his own mini festival, "Hypnorituals and Mesmemusical Miracles Hanging in the Sky: 5 Nights of Soleros and Bandoleros," at the El Cid club in Los Angeles, as well as a night of the British festival All Tomorrow's Parties. In February 2007 he headlined the "Welcome to Dreamland" bill at New York's Carnegie Hall, a lineup handpicked by ex-Talking Head David Byrne and featuring many of Banhart's peers, such as Vetiver, Vashti Bunyan, and Cibelle. A visual artist as well, Banhart's work has been exhibited at galleries all over the world, including the San Francisco Museum of Modern Art, where he had a show with Paul Klee in 2008. Banhart lives in Los Angeles.

Kevin Barker

Kevin Barker started playing guitar after seeing the film *La Bamba* at age eleven. Growing up in Washington, D.C., he took the city's DIY punk ethos to heart, founding a vinyl-only record label with his brother Derek as a sophomore in high school. While earning his MFA in film from Columbia University, he joined the band Aden as a guitarist and began recording solo under the name Currituck Co., releasing five albums (including the 2002 debut *Unpacking My Library*) and two singles. After moving to New York City, he began playing guitar and banjo on records and tours by Devendra Banhart, Joanna Newsom, Antony and the Johnsons, Vashti Bunyan, Vetiver, Espers, Ladybug Transistor, and Grass.

Bat For Lashes

Singer/songwriter, multi-instrumentalist, and visual artist Natasha Khan was born in England and spent her childhood summers in Pakistan. After earning a degree in film and music, she was working as a nursery school teacher when the inspiration for her song "Horse & I" came to her in a dream, and she began recording music as Bat For Lashes. The song served as muse for her 2006 album *Fur and Gold*, which was nominated for the Mercury Prize, and Bat For Lashes was nominated for Best British Breakthrough Act and Best British Solo Female Artist. Bat For Lashes' first North American date was 2007's SXSW festival, and the band joined Radiohead's 2008 tour. Khan lives in Brighton, England, by the sea.

Vashti Bunyan

Vashti Bunyan was born in London in 1945 and studied at the Ruskin School of Drawing and Fine Art at Oxford University, but was expelled for failing to attend classes and spending her time writing songs. At eighteen, she traveled to New York, where she discovered the music of Bob Dylan and was inspired to become a full-time musician. Returning to London, she recorded a single with Rolling Stones manager Andrew Loog Oldham, the Jagger-and-Richards-penned "Some Things Just Stick in Your Mind." This was followed by another single, "Train Song," but neither met with much attention. Bunyan subsequently decided to travel with her then boyfriend by horse and cart to the Isle of Skye to join the musician Donovan's commune. During the trip she began writing the songs that would eventually become her debut full-length album, *Just Another Diamond Day*. Produced by Joe Boyd, the album was released on Philips Records in December 1970 and met with warm reviews, but struggled to find an audience. Disappointed, Bunyan left the music industry and spent the ensuing thirty years raising her three children. During this time, entirely unbeknownst to her, the original album became a highly sought-after record, selling on eBay for as much as $2,000. *Just Another Diamond Day* was re-released on CD (with bonus tracks) in 2000, influencing a new generation of artists such as Devendra Banhart and Joanna Newsom. In 2001 Banhart wrote to Bunyan asking for advice, which led to her connection with many of the contemporary performers who cite her work as inspiration. Since then she has appeared on releases by Devendra Banhart and Animal Collective, and in 2005, recorded and released her second album, *Lookaftering*, on FatCat Records, some thirty-five years after her first. Produced by composer Max Richter and including performances by Banhart, Joanna Newsom, Adem, Kevin Barker, and Otto Hauser of Espers, *Lookaftering* was well received by critics and fans alike. In the fall of 2006, Bunyan assembled a band and embarked on a brief North American tour, performing songs from both her solo albums, as well as some unreleased material. She is currently working on a third album with Andy Cabic of Vetiver.

Cibelle

Brazilian-born musician Cibelle Cavalli Bastos's early guitar lessons led her to try her hand at piano, percussion, and singing. As a teenager, she was recruited by the Ford talent agency, and after a few commercials and a brief stint on Brazilian MTV, she returned to music full-time, singing at local clubs and jam sessions around São Paulo. Through these she met Yugoslavian ex-pat and visionary producer Suba, who recruited her to sing several tracks on his 2001 album *São Paulo Confessions*. In 2003 Cibelle released her self-titled debut and shortly thereafter moved to London, where she began working on *The Shine of Dried Electric Leaves*, featuring Brazilian musician Seu Jorge and French MC/beatboxer Spleen. Released in 2007, the album blends classic samba and bossa nova with hints of electronic percussion. The first single, "London London," is a duet with Devendra Banhart that was written by their shared musical hero, Caetano Veloso. Cibelle released the four-track EP *White Hair* in 2008.

Ariana Delawari

An Afghan/Sicilian-American, Ariana Delawari was born in Los Angeles in 1980, just after the Soviet invasion of Afghanistan. Twenty days before she was born, her father's family fled their homeland and moved to her parents' house in Los Angeles. Delawari has studied performance and visual arts throughout her life. She began playing the guitar when she was thirteen and became obsessed with protest music. Shortly after 9/11, her parents moved back to Afghanistan to help in the reconstruction of the country. Her father became the governor of the Central Bank of Afghanistan and went on to become a minister advisor to President Hamid Karzai. Her mother started working for the United Nations. Delawari began documenting her travels to Afghanistan in October 2002 in photographs and songs. She met Devendra Banhart at Coachella in 2006 after a strange encounter with a Moroccan man who'd prophesized this occurrence. Influenced by John Lennon, Jimi Hendrix, Bob Dylan, Willie Nelson, Ahmed Zahir (also known as the Afghan Elvis), and traditional Afghan music, Delawari went on to form Lion of Panjshir in July 2006, naming her group after the Persian leader Ahmad Shah Massoud, who helped drive the Soviet army out of Pakistan. A year later she and her bandmates traveled to Afghanistan, where they recorded with three Afghan elder *ustads*. She finished her debut album in Los Angeles with several guest artists and producers, including David Lynch. Delawari has performed alongside Bat For Lashes, Jonathan Wilson, and Hecuba, and in the fall of 2008 held a residency at the Los Angeles venue Tangier.

Eliza Douglas

While studying electronic arts at Bard College, New York-based musician Eliza Douglas joined the band BunnyBrains. In 2005 they opened for Devendra Banhart during his U.S. tour. Shortly after the tour ended, Douglas started playing with Banhart, and in 2006 she joined his band, touring with them for a year in the U.S. and Europe, singing through guitar pedals and playing sampler and occasional bass. At Banhart's encouragement Douglas began playing her own shows, accompanied by Banhart on guitar. She continues to pursue visual art, and has played with Matteah Baim and Telepathe and toured with Antony and the Johnsons.

Entrance

Born in Baltimore, Maryland, Guy Blakeslee became an obsessive music fan and lover of art and poetry at a very early age. At nine, influenced by a babysitter who turned him on to skateboarding, hip-hop, and punk rock, he began teaching himself to play his brother's guitar, flipping the instrument upside-down (Blakeslee is left-handed), inventing his own tunings, and writing his own songs. At fourteen, he started playing in bands with older kids and helping book and organize shows at all-ages venues in Baltimore, putting up touring hardcore bands in his mother's basement and making zines full of collage and stream-of-consciousness writings. At the age of seventeen, he went on his first tour, playing bass with the band Convocation Of, which initiated him into the life of a traveling musician. On September 11, 2001, he quit the band and went solo, calling himself Entrance and taking inspiration from recordings of American blues, folk, and gospel from the 1920s and '30s. In 2002 he opened for Will Oldham on a West Coast tour, where he met Devendra Banhart, subsequently touring the United States with him. His first record as Entrance, *The Kingdom of Heaven Must Be Taken by Storm*, was released in 2002, followed by an international tour with Cat Power and the EP *Careless Love*. His 2004 album *Wandering Stranger* featured Tommy Rouse on drums and Paz Lenchantin on violin and piano. After a tour of the United States and Europe with the Yeah Yeah Yeahs, Blakeslee settled in Los Angeles and began writing the rock opera *Prayer of Death* with drummer Derek James and Lenchantin, which was released in 2006. He is now playing and recording with Lenchantin and James as the Entrance Band. Blakeslee lives in Laurel Canyon with his partner, Maximilla Lukacs.

Espers

Formed in 2003 in Philadelphia by singer/songwriters Greg Weeks and Meg Baird and guitarist Brooke Sientinsons, Espers later expanded to a sextet including percussionist Otto Hauser, cellist Helena Espvall, and bassist Christopher Smith. Taking the psychedelic folk and progressive music of the late '60s onward as their jumping-off point, Espers followed the tradition of underground art and music collectives formed around common interests in forwarding the complex aesthetics of this era. A self-titled album was released in 2004, followed by an EP of covers, traditional songs, and originals (*The Weed Tree*) in 2005. Their second full-length album, *II*, was released in 2006 on Drag City. Espers has shared the stage with British folk luminaries Bert Jansch, Michael Hurley, Vashti Bunyan, and the Incredible String Band, as well as contemporaries Brightblack Morning Light, Devendra Banhart, Sir Richard Bishop, and Vetiver.

Feathers

Comprising eight musicians, the Vermont-based collective Feathers is a leaderless group of songwriters. Beginning in 2004 as the duo of Kurt Weisman and Kyle Thomas, the band gradually grew through a circle of old and new friends, as musicians Meara O'Reilly, Ruth Garbus, Shayna Kipping, Jordan Morris, Greg Petrovato, and Asa Irons all became members. Feathers began playing extensively around New England before embarking on national tours with Smog and Espers. They self-released a series of EPs and CD singles, which they sold at their live shows. Drawing inspiration from art and literature, the group's primarily guitar-based songs are colored by a wide range of instruments, including harp, sitar, and clarinet. Carefully arranged vocal harmonies also figure prominently in their writing. Recorded in Kyle Thomas's bedroom in Vermont, Feathers' eponymous debut album was released on Andy Cabic and Devendra Banhart's Gnomonsong label in 2006. Feathers also contributed to several tracks on Devendra Banhart's album *Cripple Crow*.

Ruthann Friedman

Born in the Bronx in 1944, Ruthann Friedman started playing Hoot Nights at the Troubador in Los Angeles when she was sixteen. During the Great Hippie Migration, she sang up and down the coast of California. In San Francisco, Friedman lived with members of the Jefferson Airplane in Haight-Ashbury, sang with Country Joe & the Fish at the Avalon Ballroom, and learned the pleasures of Southern Comfort from Janis Joplin while hunting for hot smokey links in the Fillmore District. While living in David Crosby's home in Beverly Glenn Canyon, Friedman wrote the song "Windy"; when the Association recorded it in 1967, the song's success gave her the freedom to do whatever she wanted. She released her first solo album, *Constant Companion*, on A&M Records in 1970. Married with two daughters, Friedman openly shares her gratitude to Devendra Banhart, who, as she says, "brought me out of obscurity" by publicly declaring his enthusiasm for her music, and inviting her to perform in 2006 at the Banhart-curated mini festival "Hypnorituals and Mesmemusical Miracles Hanging in the Sky: 5 Nights of Soleros and Bandoleros" alongside Feathers, Jana Hunter, the Entrance Band, and Adam Tullie. *Constant Companion* was re-released in 2006 on the San Francisco label Water, followed by *Hurried Life*, a compilation of Friedman's rare and previously unreleased home recordings from 1965–1971. Now residing in Venice, California, Friedman continues to tour and record music.

Noah Georgeson

Noah Georgeson was born in Marin County, California, and was raised in Nevada City. His mother, Mary, has played music and sung her whole life, and at the age of sixteen was offered a record contract with Decca Records, which she declined out of shyness. His father, Andrew, a boxer and Navy man turned yogi, plays flute. Noah has two brothers, one older, Jon Eric, and one younger, Amar, who lives in China and plays classical piano. As a teenager, Noah played in various punk bands and took classical guitar lessons, where he met Gyan Riley. The two would practice and write together at Gyan's parents' ranch, where they would listen to Gyan's father, composer Terry Riley, improvising on piano. After studying classical guitar in college, Noah turned his focus to music composition, earning a bachelor's degree from San Francisco State University and a master's degree from Mills College. After finishing school, Noah produced, recorded, sang, and played guitar on Joanna Newsom's 2004 debut album *The Milk-Eyed Mender*, later touring with Newsom and with Georgeson's own band, the Pleased. In autumn 2004 he began touring as a guitarist with Devendra Banhart, and in January 2005 the two moved to Woodstock, New York, to record *Cripple Crow*, which Noah produced, engineered, and performed on. The rest of 2005 was spent touring with Banhart, though he also found time to produce Mason Jennings' album *Boneclouds* and arrange strings and play on Vetiver's *To Find Me Gone*. In 2006 he moved with Banhart to Venice, California, where he produced albums by Constance Verluca and Bert Jansch, and released his solo debut, *Find Shelter*, that same year. Much of 2007 was spent in Topanga Canyon, California, writing and recording Banhart's *Smokey Rolls Down Thunder Canyon*, which he produced, engineered, co-wrote, and played on. He also produced the self-titled debut album *Little Joy*, and upon finishing joined the band. He currently resides in Topanga Canyon and is working on a second solo record.

Benjamin Oak Goodman

Benjamin Oak Goodman was raised in the Victorian gold-mining hills of Nevada City, California. After spending time in San Francisco and New York City, he now lives in the Northern California coastal mountain town of Jenner. An independent recording artist, Goodman writes, performs, and records in a minimalist style. His releases include *Yes, My Heart* (2007) along with a series of DIY singles and EPs, and he is featured on the Grass Roots Records compilation *Family Album*. A multi-instrumentalist, he played drums and percussion on Devendra Banhart's *Smokey Rolls Down Thunder Canyon* and has performed and/or recorded with Noah Georgeson, Alina Estelle Hardin, Night Court, and Alela Diane.

Hecuba

A project created by Isabelle Albuquerque and Jon Beasley, Hecuba was formed in New York City in 2003, when the pair met while working on a film about alien abduction. Their collaboration evolved into a science-fiction music project called Aldiss (after the science-fiction writer Brian Aldiss), later becoming the experimental and eclectic group Hecuba. Beasley was born and raised in Montgomery, Alabama, where his mother sang in the church choir and he was an organist. He played in several bands before becoming interested in making electronic-based music and programming beats. Albuquerque was born in Los Angeles and spent much of her childhood traveling with her artist mother to sacred sites across the globe, where they installed art pieces associated with the Earthworks movement. Albuquerque met Devendra Banhart when they were neighbors in Encinal Canyon; they later attended high school together. Hecuba's live appearances often incorporate aspects of performance art and feature guest performers. The band's debut EP, *Dear Sir*, was released in 2008. Albuquerque and Beasley live in Los Angeles.

Jana Hunter

Jana Hunter was born and raised in Pantego, Texas, in 1978. After spending much of her youth training as a classical violinist, she began to pursue songwriting as a teenager, performing at open mics and local house parties. She moved to New York City at age eighteen, then back and forth between New York and Houston before settling at age twenty-nine in Baltimore. Her debut album, 2005's *Blank Unstaring Heirs of Doom*, was the debut release on Andy Cabic and Devendra Banhart's Gnomonsong label, and was followed in 2007 by *There's No Home* and its accompanying EP, *Carrion*. Hunter has performed and/or recorded with numerous bands and artists, including Castanets, Matteah Baim, Metallic Falcons, Phosphorescent, and CocoRosie.

Michael Hurley

Born in 1941, Michael Hurley grew up in Bucks County, Pennsylvania. He discovered country music at a young age and left home when he was seventeen, hitchhiking to New Orleans, New York, and Mexico. Inspired by folk music, blues, and rock 'n' roll, he learned to play the guitar and began writing his first songs, recording his debut album, *First Songs*, in 1965 on the same reel-to-reel machine that had taped Leadbelly's last sessions. In the late '70s Hurley made three albums for Rounder Records. His 1976 recording, *Have Moicy*, a collaboration with the Unholy Modal Rounders (so renamed due to the absence of group member Steve Weber) and Jeffrey Frederick & the Clamtones, was named "the greatest folk rock album of the rock era" by the *Village Voice*'s Robert Christgau. In the late '90s, Hurley toured with Son Volt and received high praise from younger performers like Lucinda Williams, Vic Chesnutt, Calexico, and Cat Power. On his latest album, *Ancestral Swamp*, released in 2007 on Devendra Banhart and Andy Cabic's label Gnomonsong, Hurley is backed by longtime associate David Reisch of the Holy Modal Rounders along with Tara Jane O'Neill and Lewi Longmire. Hurley has played shows with Vetiver, Matteah Baim, and Entrance, and Vetiver and Espers have covered his songs.

Bert Jansch

PhaseSinger/songwriter and guitarist Bert Jansch was born in 1942 in Glasgow, Scotland, but was raised in Edinburgh. As a teenager, he bought an acoustic guitar and spent much of his spare time at local folk club the Howff. In 1963 he traveled to London with his Edinburgh flatmate Robin Williamson, who would go on to form the Incredible String Band in 1966. Jansch recorded his self-titled first album on a reel-to-reel tape deck with a borrowed guitar. Upon its release in April 1965, the album caused a sensation with Jansch's innovative guitar technique and songwriting, and notably popularized the Davey Graham instrumental "Anji." Jansch went on to record over twenty-five albums, and his musical influence can be clearly heard in the work of other British guitarists of the mid to late '60s, including Nick Drake, Ian Anderson, and Jimmy Page. In 2001 Jansch received a lifetime achievement award at the BBC Radio 2 Folk Awards. In 2006 he released the album *Black Swan*, produced by Noah Georgeson and including collaborations with Devendra Banhart, Otto Hauser (Espers, Vetiver), Helena Espvall (Espers), and Kevin Barker. Later that year he received the MOJO Merit Award at the MOJO Honors List ceremony. Jansch is also a member of the group Pentangle.

Little Joy

The Los Angeles–based band Little Joy comprises members Binki Shapiro, Rodrigo Amarante, and Fabrizio Moretti. Amarante (Los Hermanos) and Moretti (the Strokes) met in 2006 at a music festival in Lisbon, Portugal, where they were both performing, and discussed collaborating in the future. In 2007, when he was in Los Angeles to record with Devendra Banhart on *Smokey Rolls Down Thunder Canyon*, Amarante renewed his friendship with Moretti. They were later joined by Binki Shapiro, who was introduced to the pair through mutual acquaintances and encouraged them to focus on their music. Soon after, the three began writing original music as a band. By the end of 2007 they had moved into a house in Echo Park to demo songs, and with the help of producer Noah Georgeson, who had recorded Banhart's music, they soon finished their self-titled debut, *Little Joy*, which was released in 2008 on Rough Trade Records. The following fall, Little Joy toured the West Coast with Megapuss and Entrance.

Megapuss

Megapuss began as a band that wrote only song titles, not songs. Eventually founding members Gregory Rogove and Devendra Banhart put music to their titles and composed most of the songs that would comprise their debut album, *Surfing*, while on tour in support of Banhart's record *Smokey Rolls Down Thunder Canyon*. In March 2008 they recorded *Surfing* in a few days in a cabin in Los Angeles, using mostly first takes. For the song "Theme from Hollywood," they enlisted the help of Fabrizio Moretti of the Strokes. Moretti has since become a regular member of the band, and plays drums for their live performances. *Surfing* was released by Neil Young's label Vapor Records. In the fall of 2008, Megapuss toured the West Coast together with Entrance and Moretti's group Little Joy.

Joanna Newsom

Born in 1982 and raised in the tiny town of Nevada City, California, Joanna Newsom began playing harp at the age of eight, learning Celtic, Senegalese, Venezuelan, and Western classical harp. She studied composition and creative writing at Mills College in Oakland, California, where she met musician Noah Georgeson. In 2001 Newsom played keyboards in the San Francisco–based band the Pleased, which included Georgeson and Luckey Remington. She self-released an EP of her first home recordings, *Walnut Whales*, in 2002. Initially given out only to friends, the EP soon caught outside attention. Newsom was subsequently signed to Drag City and released her full-length debut, *The Milk-Eyed Mender*, which was produced by Georgeson, in 2004. Later that year, she toured the United States with Devendra Banhart and Europe with Smog. Newsom's second record, *Ys*, came out in late 2006, and included collaborators Bill Callahan, Steve Albini, Jim O'Rourke, and Van Dyke Parks. The album became one of the year's most critically acclaimed releases, and Newsom spent the end of 2006 and early 2007 touring in support of it, embarking on an Orchestral Tour featuring orchestral arrangements by Van Dyke Parks and including performances with the London Symphony Orchestra, Australia's Symphony Orchestra, Chicago Symphony Orchestra, and the Los Angeles Philharmonic. Newsom has performed in such venues as the Royal Albert Hall, Sydney Opera House, and the Walt Disney Concert Hall. In the spring of 2007, she released the EP *Joanna Newsom & the Ys Street Band*, which was recorded and mixed in three days. She has also played on records by Smog, Vetiver, and Vashti Bunyan.

Pete Newsom

Pete Newsom was raised by a musical family in the town of Nevada City, California. His parents and two sisters played cello, piano, guitar, and harp. Newsom began playing drums at age eleven and the piano at twenty-four. In 2003 his sister Joanna introduced him to Devendra Banhart. While Newsom was visiting New York in 2006, Banhart asked him if he'd like to sit in on piano for his show at the Hammerstein Ballroom. This led to more performances with Banhart, including playing at the Bridge School Benefit in California in 2006 and Carnegie Hall in early 2007. Newsom also joined Banhart's band for the recording and touring of the album *Smokey Rolls Down Thunder Canyon*. He is currently writing his own music and living in the Northern California foothills.

Linda Perhacs

Born in Santa Monica, California, Linda Perhacs began writing music at the age of six. In the early '70s, while working as a dental hygienist in a Beverly Hills periodontal office, she played a tape for friend and dental patient Leonard Rosenman that she made herself on a cassette recorder in the kitchen of her Topanga Canyon home. An accomplished avant-garde composer and film director, Rosenman found her work promising, and subsequently recorded her album *Parallelograms*. Unfortunately, the record received little notice and quickly went out of print. Perhacs returned to her career as a dental hygienist and gave little thought to her music until 2000, when Michael Piper, founder of the collectable/reissue record label the Wild Places, contacted her to let her know the album was considered to be one of the great lost records of the '70s and was cherished by those fans lucky enough to find it. *Parallelograms* was re-released in 2005 as *Parallelograms Deux II*. Perhacs also collaborated with Devendra Banhart, a devoted fan who had tracked her down. After her music was featured in the Daft Punk movie *Electroma*, Perhacs gained the attention of a new generation of fans. Still living in Topanga Canyon, Perhacs is working on a new record.

Priestbird

Priestbird comprises the musicians Danny Bensi, Saunder Jurriaans, and Gregory Rogove, who had formerly performed and recorded as the instrumental trio Tarantula A.D. Following a change in musical direction from cinematic, classical-influenced instrumentals to song-based, psychedelic rock, the band added vocals and renamed themselves Priestbird. They have played with Pearl Jam, Dungen, the Sword, Grizzly Bear, and Devendra Banhart. Their debut album, *In Your Time*, was released in 2007.

Ramblin' Jack Elliott

Born Elliott Charles Adnopoz in Brooklyn, New York, Elliott ran away when he was fifteen years old to join the J. E. Rodeo in the mid-1940s. It was there that he saw his first "singing cowboy," a rodeo clown who sang songs on guitar and banjo. Elliott traveled with the rodeo for three months before his parents tracked him down and he was sent home. Back at home, Elliott taught himself how to play guitar and started busking. Around this time, he met folksinger Woody Guthrie, and soon became his protégé and close friend. Elliott and Guthrie wandered the country over the next five years playing music together off and on. In 1954 they drove to Los Angeles, California, where Elliott met his wife-to-be, June Hammerstein, through her then husband, James Dean. After relocating with June to England in the mid-1950s, Elliott was surprised to find that American rural music had become Top 40. He toured Great Britain and Europe and had a lasting effect on the music scene abroad, making three folk albums for the British label Topic by 1960. Returning to the United States, Elliott discovered that he had become well known within the folk scene; he went on to release more than forty EPs, LPs, and CDs. In 1995 his album *South Coast* earned him his first Grammy, and he was awarded the National Medal of Arts in 1998. Elliott's flatpicking guitar style and command of Guthrie's material as well as early American roots music such as country, blues, bluegrass, and folk have earned him a special place in musical history. Over the years Ramblin' Jack has acquired an extensive list of musician friends and admirers, including fan Devendra Banhart, who invited Elliott to play at the 2005 British festival All Tomorrow's Parties, and Jonathan Wilson, with whom he played a show in Los Angeles in 2006.

Luckey Remington

The son of a lumberjack and a daughter of the Gold Beach, Luckey Remington was born in Eugene, Oregon. From 2001 to 2004 he wrote and performed with the Pleased, which included members Noah Georgeson and Joanna Newsom, and recorded one full-length album with the band, *Don't Make Things*. Remington has toured and recorded bass with Devendra Banhart since 2005, and currently lives in Paris, France, where he makes short films and is producing an album of his own work.

Rio en Medio

Most of the material that comprises *The Bride of Dynamite*, Rio en Medio's first album, was written by Danielle Stech-Homsy upon her return from a trip to Russia, where she had been translating poetry. Recorded on her own with no intention of commercial release, the music features Stech-Homsy's ukelele, layered vocals, samples, electronics, and other sounds as well as texts from William Blake, Paul Eluard, John Ashbery, and a 1920s Baghdad travelogue. The songs were overheard by Devendra Banhart, who pleaded for her to release them; the album subsequently came out on Gnomonsong in 2007 with contributions by musicians including Andy Cabic, who provided production assistance. Following its release, Rio en Medio began playing in New York with accompanists Justin Riddle and Christian Lee. The band's second album, *Frontier* (2008), was written as a series of interrelated poems that were later set to music and recorded in Stech-Homsy's home in northern New Mexico.

Spleen

Born in Paris, France, in 1982 to a family of Cameroonian origin, Spleen grew up in a strict household with his three siblings. He became increasingly interested in music and art, and as a teenager found himself in the middle of the Parisian music scene, where he participated in improvised jam sessions with his musician friends. Singing in both French and English, Spleen began to mix gospel, poetry, hip-hop, and soul music with vocal beatboxing and vocal blues. While attending a show at a jazz club in Saint-Germain-des-Prés in 2004, Spleen met Bianca and Sierra Casady of CocoRosie. He went on to collaborate with CocoRosie on their second record, *Noah's Arc*, and toured extensively with them throughout Europe and the United States. During this time he met fellow musicians Antony and the Johnsons, Devendra Banhart, and Cibelle. In 2005 Spleen released his first solo record, *She Was a Girl*, and shortly after produced and released the compilation *The Black & White Skins Vol. 1*, with tracks from artists including Antony and the Johnsons, Devendra Banhart, Jana Hunter, Bat For Lashes, and Danielle Stech-Homsy. Spleen collaborated with Cibelle on her 2007 release *The Shine of Dried Electric Leaves*, performing on the duet "Mad Man Song." In the fall of 2008, Spleen released his second solo record, *Comme un Enfant*, on Remark/Universal Records.

Becky Stark

Becky Stark grew up in Maryland, just outside of Washington, D.C. When she was eleven years old, a classical music teacher took an interest in her singing and worked with her for the next five years, until she was told that her future as a classical singer was limited by her tiny ribcage. She soon learned about another side of music after seeing the D.C. punk band Fugazi in concert. While attending Brown University, Stark began writing and performing punk operettas. After college, she continued performing as part of Providence's music scene, finding particular success with her play *Birdsongs of the Bauharoque*, which was popular enough to spur a national tour in 2003. Stark played the main character, a bird-woman named Lavender Diamond, whose job was to invent peace on earth. After moving to Los Angeles, Stark formed the band Lavender Diamond with drummer Ron Regé Jr., pianist Steve Gregoropoulos, and guitarist Devon Williams. Their debut recording, the four-song EP *The Cavalry of Light*, was released in 2005. Over the next year the band recorded with Vetiver, Brightblack Morning Light, and Devendra Banhart and released the full-length album *Imagine Our Love* in 2007.

Adam Tullie

Born in 1982 in Boston, Massachusetts, Adam Tullie has lived in Southern California most of his life. At age seven he was given a sombrero and an acoustic guitar from his parents as a birthday present. He spent teenage days surfing the ocean, skateboarding around San Juan Capistrano, making works on paper, and painting on walls. In 2001 Tullie moved to Los Angeles to attend art school, but left shortly thereafter to travel through Europe. After returning to the United States, Tullie began to record short, improvised songs on a four-track in his Skid Row room in downtown Los Angeles. In 2005 he founded the clothing line Cavern with design partner Angeline Rivas, and together they have collaborated with Devendra Banhart and Beck on visual projects and designing the artists' merchandise. In 2006 Tullie performed an acoustic guitar-driven set with his friend Elijah Forrest at the Banhart-curated mini festival "Hypnorituals and Mesmemusical Miracles Hanging in the Sky: 5 Nights of Soleros and Bandoleros" at El Cid in Los Angeles. He also wrote and recorded the score to a short film by Maximilla Lukacs revolving around Cavern's Spring/Summer 2008 collection.

Vetiver

Growing up in northern Virginia, Andy Cabic spent a few years in Greensboro, North Carolina, playing guitar, writing music, and recording as a member of the rock band Raymond Brake. After moving to San Francisco in 1998, Cabic joined the rock band Tussle, simultaneously recruiting local musicians and friends including Alissa Anderson, Otto Hauser, Carmen Biggers, Kevin Barker, Sanders Trippe, Brent Dunn, and Devendra Banhart to form Vetiver. Vetiver's self-titled debut album was released in 2004 to high critical praise. Following its release, Cabic toured extensively with the band and various incarnations of Banhart's touring ensemble. In 2006 Vetiver released their second album, *To Find Me Gone*. Vetiver has toured and collaborated with Vashti Bunyan, the Shins, Michael Hurley, and Joanna Newsom and played at the February 2007 "Welcome to Dreamland" show at Carnegie Hall in New York. In 2008 the band released *Thing of the Past*, a set of covers of songs by some of Cabic's favorite artists.

Warpaint

Los Angeles-based Warpaint is made up of sisters Jenny Lee Lindberg and Shannyn Sossamon and their childhood friends Theresa Wayman and Emily Kokal. The pairs met and befriended each other at a jam session on Valentine's Day 2004 at their friend Dave Orlando's music studio in Hollywood. Only Kokal had ever played music in a band before. The group began playing together regularly and formed Warpaint, traveling to Canada to write material. Returning to Los Angeles, they moved into a house in Los Feliz, where they continued to write and began playing shows to share their experiment with their friends. After recording their first EP, *Exquisite Corpse*, which was released in September 2008, Sossamon left the band and was replaced by Orlando. Warpaint has performed with Entrance, Ben Goodman, Megapuss, and Hecuba.

Jonathan Wilson

Musician and producer Jonathan Wilson was born in Spindale, North Carolina. In 1995 he founded the band Muscadine with Benji Hughes. He recorded a solo album, *Frankie Ray*, in 2007, which received positive reviews but was never officially released. He is working on a new record featuring guest appearances by Barry Goldberg, Chris Robinson, Gary Louris, Andy Cabic, Otto Hauser, Josh Grange, Gary Mallaber, Z Berg, Adam McDougall, and Johnathan Rice. Wilson has recorded with Elvis Costello, Jenny Lewis, Farmer Dave Scher, and Phil Lesh, among others. The private jam sessions he hosts at his home in Laurel Canyon have received international attention for their unique "Canyon Folk" feel, and have included Cabic, Louris, the Black Crowes, Wilco, Electric Flag, Paul Butterfield Blues Band, Jakob Dylan, Entrance, Jenny Lewis, Jonathan Rice, David Rawlings, members of the Jayhawks, the Cars, Pearl Jam, and members of Van Morrison, Bruce Springsteen, and Steve Miller's bands.

ACKNOWLEDGMENTS

I would like to acknowledge and extend my heartfelt gratitude to the following persons who have made the completion of this book possible:

Barry, Denise, and Michael Dukoff, for their love and support. Autumn de Wilde, for her mentoring and friendship. Josh Loucka for his understanding and encouragement. Steve Mockus for believing in me.

To all of those who worked and contributed to this book. Megan Steinman and Eric Roinestad for their incredible design talent and undying dedication to this book. Jen Jenkins, Eleni Peters, and Giant Artists. Steve Block, Brian Greenberg, Joey Hinkle, and all of Paris Photo Lab. Gary Held. Jacob Gardner, Becca Cohen, and Erin Thacker at Chronicle Books.

Most especially to my family and friends. William and Sally Feathers, Lois "Big Lolo" Wherman, Gale Wherman. Ashley Furnival, Victoria Asher, Sandy Ganzer, and Sarah Foster. Kevin Whitman, Donald and Leslie Furnival, Kate and Laura Mullevy, Kate Betuel, Maria Eugenia Risquez, Loring Baker. Alex, Brittany, and Justine Parkin. Bill Bixler, Carla Bowmansmith, Jennifer Gonzales, Peter and Wendy Asher, Brandon Goddard, Brandon Lehr, George Ducker, Arrow de Wilde, Wynn Lewis, Antonio Ballatore, Kyle Stevenson, Matt Kane, Gina Mundy, Shirley Kurata, Magda Woliski, Alison Bernier, Amy Jo Diaz, Joel Graves, Erin Turnmire, Katie Casey, Samantha Rapp, Liz Hart, Howard Wuelfing, and Dean Correa. Lookout Management, Elliot Roberts, Aram Goldberg, Gio Cianci, and Bonnie Levetin.

And above all, thank you to all the artists in the book.

In loving memory of Vivian Ray Dukoff.

LIST OF PHOTOGRAPHS

L–R: Fabrizio Moretti, Binki Shapiro, Spirit,
Devendra Banhart, Greg Rogove, Noah
Georgeson, and Rodrigo Amarante
Big Sur, CA
September 2008

Matteah Baim
Malibu, CA
January 2007

Devendra Banhart
Philadelphia, PA
October 2007

(L–R) Noah Georgeson, Greg Rogove, Lila Stowell,
Luckey Remington, Butchy Fuego, Devendra
Banhart, Matteah Baim, and Pete Newsom
Sixth & I Historic Synagogue, Washington, DC
October 2007

Devendra Banhart
Devendra's home/studio, Topanga, CA
April 2007

Writings by Devendra Banhart and
Matteah Baim
Devendra's home/studio, Topanga, CA
March 2007

Devendra Banhart
Devendra's home/studio, Topanga, CA
March 2007

Natasha Kahn of Bat For Lashes
Natasha's home, Brooklyn, NY
February 2008

City God and *Forest Sun* by Natasha Kahn
2007

Guy Blakeslee
Guy's home, Los Angeles, CA
May 2008

Jonathan Wilson
Jonathan's home, Los Angeles, CA
August 2008

Fabrizio Moretti and Binki Shapiro of Little Joy
Los Angeles, CA
July 2008

Vashti Bunyan
Vashti's home, Edinburgh, Scotland
April 2008

Before and *After*
by Whyn Lewis (Vashti Bunyan's daughter)
April 2008
Courtesy of Portal Gallery (London)

Feathers: (L–R) Kurt Weisman, Ruth Garbus, and Kyle Thomas
Brattleboro, VT
May 2008

Greg Rogove
Chemin de Halage, Toulouse, France
November 2008

Alissa Anderson and Andy Cabic of Vetiver
Philadelphia, PA
September 2007

Devendra's desk
Devendra's home/studio, Topanga, CA
March 2007

Priestbird: (L–R) Danny Bensi, Saunder Jurriaans, and Greg Rogove
Priestbird's recording studio, Woodstock, NY
March 2008

Ariana Delawari of Lion of Panjshir
San Luis Obispo, CA
March 2008

Kyle Thomas's studio
Brattleboro, VT
May 2008

Danielle Stech-Homsy of Rio en Medio
Arcadia, CA
March 2008

Benjamin Oak Goodman
Topanga, CA
February 2007

Luckey Remington
Topanga, CA
February 2007

Guy Blakeslee of Entrance
Canyon behind Guy's home, Los Angeles, CA
May 2008

Devendra Banhart and his father, Loring Baker
Topanga, CA
June 2007

Andy Cabic of Vetiver
Camber Sands, England
May 2006

(L–R) Andy Cabic, Eliza Douglas, Otto Hauser, Noah Georgeson, Devendra Banhart, and Luckey Remington
Camber Sands, England
May 2006

Natasha Kahn of Bat For Lashes and Will Lemon
Camber Sands, England
May 2006

Linda Perhacs
Topanga, CA
May 2008

Cibelle
Abney Park Cemetery, London, England
April 2008

Matteah Baim, cover for *Death of the Sun*
Malibu, CA
January 2007

Matteah Baim
Malibu, CA
January 2007

Bert Jansch
Bridge School Benefit, Mountain View, CA
October 2006

All Tomorrow's Parties festival 2006 lineup,
curated by Devendra Banhart
Camber Sands, England, May 2006

Devendra Banhart
Outside Lands Festival, Golden Gate Park,
San Francisco, August 2008

Devendra Banhart
Barcelona, Spain
November 2007

(L–R) Andy Cabic, Devendra Banhart, Noah
Georgeson, and Otto Hauser
All Tomorrow's Parties festival, Camber Sands,
England
May 2006

Marquee
The Fillmore, Philadelphia, PA
September 2007

Noah Georgeson and Pete Newsom
El Rey Theater, Los Angeles, CA
November 2006

Rodrigo Amarante, Fabrizio Moretti, and
Binki Shapiro
Troubadour, Los Angeles, CA
September 2008

Spleen
Carnegie Hall, New York, NY
February, 2007

Rouge—Get Rich! by Spleen
Undated

Isabelle Albuquerque of Hecuba
Orpheum Theater, Los Angeles, CA
October 2007

Neil Young playing "Rockin' in the Free World"
Bridge School Benefit, Mountain View, CA
October 2006

(L–R) Jo Mango, Vashti Bunyan, and
Andy Cabic
Carnegie Hall, New York, NY
February 2007

(L–R) Noah Georgeson, Greg Rogove, Devendra
Banhart, Gio Cianci, Andy Cabic, and Luckey
Remington
Sixth & I Historic Synagogue, Washington, DC
October 2007

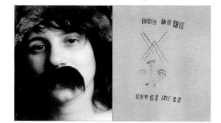

Matteah Baim
Matteah, Devendra, and Noah's former home.
Venice, CA
July 2006

Untitled by Matteah Baim
2008

Isabelle Albuquerque and Devendra Banhart
Orpheum Theatre, Los Angeles, CA
October 2007

Joanna Newsom
El Rey Theater, Los Angeles, CA
November 2006

Matteah Baim resting at the side of the stage
while Devendra performs
All Tomorrow's Parties festival, Camber Sands,
England
May 2006

Devendra Banhart and Kevin Barker
Los Angeles, CA
April 2008

Ariana Delawari
Madonna Inn, San Luis Obispo, CA
March 2008

Devendra Banhart
Joy Eslava Theater, Madrid, Spain
November 2007

Noah Georgeson
All Tomorrow's Parties festival, Camber Sands,
England
May 2006

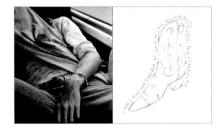

Devendra Banhart asleep in the van
London, England

Untitled (Boot) by Vashti Bunyan
2008

Devendra Banhart on Jim Morrison's couch.
wearing Mick Jagger's suit and Bob Dylan's hat
Devendra's home/studio, Topanga, CA
February 2007

Devendra Banhart
Sala Apolo, Barcelona, Spain
September 2007

Adam Tullie
Los Angeles, CA
May 2008

Cosmic Pharaoh by Adam Tullie
2007

Michael Hurley warming up before a performance with Matteah Baim
McCabe's Guitar Shop, Santa Monica, CA
February 2008

(L–R) Otto Hauser, Devendra Banhart, Eliza Douglas, Luckey Remington, and Noah Georgeson
Bridge School Benefit, Mountain View, CA
October 2006

Eliza Douglas
Grand Ballroom, New York, NY
September 2007

Espers: (L–R) Meg Baird, Brooke Sietinsons, Helena Espvall, Greg Weeks, and Chris Smith
Philadelphia, PA
March 2008

Devendra Banhart getting tattoo of bandmate's initials
Philadelphia, PA
September 2007

View from Devendra's home/studio,
Topanga, CA
February 2007

Devendra Banhart
The Fillmore, Philadelphia, PA
September 2007

(L–R) Devendra Banhart, Greg Rogove, and Noah Georgeson
Sala Apolo, Barcelona, Spain
September 2007

(L–R) Noah Georgeson, Devendra Banhart, Pete Newsom, and models
Italian *Vogue* photo shoot, New York, NY
February 2007

Devendra Banhart
Italian *Vogue* photo shoot, New York, NY
February 2007

Devendra Banhart with model
Italian *Vogue* photo shoot, New York, NY
February 2007

Isabelle Albuquerque and Jon Beasley of Hecuba
Los Angeles, CA
December 2007

Monkey Painting by Jon Beasley
2006

Devendra's accordion
Devendra's home/studio, Topanga, CA
February 2007

(L–R) Beau Raymond, Luckey Remington, Pete
Newsom, Greg Rogove, Devendra Banhart,
Noah Georgeson and Andy Cabic, as the
Cockettes
West Hollywood, CA
June 2007

(L–R) Beau Raymond, Pete Newsom, Devendra
Banhart, Luckey Remington, Andy Cabic, Greg
Rogove, and Noah Georgeson as the Cockettes
West Hollywood, CA
June 2007

Devendra Banhart
West Hollywood, CA
June 2007

Jana Hunter
Baltimore, MD
March 2008

Devendra Banhart of Megapuss
Los Angeles, CA
March 2008

Greg Rogove of Megapuss
Los Angeles, CA
March 2008

Natasha Kahn
Natasha's home, Brooklyn, NY
February 2008

Buck's head
Devendra's home/studio, Topanga, CA
February 2007

Ramblin' Jack Elliott
Devendra's hotel room, Camber Sands, England
May 2006

Devendra Banhart
Chicago, IL
July 2006

Mandala by Warpaint
2007

Warpaint: (L–R) Theresa Wayman, David
Orlando, Jenny Lee Lindberg, and Emily Kokal
Emily's home, Los Angeles, CA
July 2008

Devendra Banhart and Noah Georgeson
Lille, France
November 2007

Rodrigo Amarante and Devendra Banhart
Devendra's home/studio, Topanga, CA
February 2007

Ruthann Friedman
Devendra's home/studio, Topanga, CA
February 2007

Becky Stark of Lavender Diamond
Los Angeles, CA
January 2008

Studio wall
Devendra's home/studio, Topanga, CA
February 2007

Binki Shapiro of Little Joy
Los Angeles, CA
January 2008

Art by Devendra Banhart
Devendra's home/studio, Topanga, CA
February 2007

Devendra Banhart
Devendra's home/studio, Topanga, CA
February 2007

(top row, L–R) Alina Hardin as Noah Georgeson,
Noah Georgeson, Rodrigo Amarante as Andy Cabic,
Benjamin Oak Goodman as Luckey Remington,
Luckey Remington; (seated bottom row, L–R)
Beau Raymond, Devendra Banhart, Pete Newsom,
Ashley Furnival as Greg Rogove
Devendra's home, February 2007

Lo and Obi
Carnegie Hall, New York NY
February 2007

Devendra Banhart with fans
Chicago, IL
July 2006

(L–R) Noah Georgeson, Devendra Banhart,
Binki Shapiro, Greg Rogove,
Rodrigo Amarante, Fabrizio Moretti
Big Sur, CA
September 2008

This book is complemented by a compilation of tracks provided by the artists included in Family.
To download the songs, and to learn more about the artists, please visit www.chroniclebooks.com/family
and enter the code BV45JH7

FAMILY

"I Know No Pardon"
Vetiver
Written by Andy Cabic/Published by Vetiverse (BMI),
Administered by Domino Publishing Company of America, Inc. (BMI).
Courtesy of DiCristina Records.

"You and Me"
Kevin Barker
Written by Kevin Barker.
Courtesy of Gnomonsong.

"All I Know"
Ruthann Friedman
Written by Ruthann Friedman.
Courtesy of Ruthann Friedman.

"Wayward"
Vashti Bunyan, with Devendra Banhart, Otto Hauser, Kevin Baker, Adem, and Max Richter
Written by Vashti Bunyan/Published by Spinneysongs (PRS),
Administered by Domino Publishing Company of America Inc. (BMI).
Courtesy of DiCristina Records.

"We Came Home"
Ariana Delawari
Written by Ariana Delawari.
Courtesy of Ariana Delawari.

"The Magic"
Hecuba
Written by Jon Beasley and Isabelle Albuquerque.
Courtesy of Hecuba.

"Surfing"
Megapuss
Written by Devendra Banhart/Chrysalis Songs (BMI).
All Rights Reserved/Goldennegress (BMI) and Greg Rogove/G-rexx Music (ASCAP).
Courtesy of Vapor Records.

"Pagoda"
Matteah Baim
Written by Matteah Baim.
Courtesy of DiCristina Records.